Duke and the Tag

By Cameron Macintosh

June and Mum were at home.

"June, let's walk Duke," said Mum.

"Duke, come!" called June.

But Duke did not come.

“That gate is not shut!” said June.

“Duke must have got out!”

"Duke has a tag
on his neck," said Mum.
"We can use my phone
to find him."

“Duke is that red dot,” said Mum.

“He is at the lake on Mule Slope!” said June. “I hope we find him!”

Mum and June drove to Mule Slope to hunt for Duke.

Duke froze.

He could see Mum and June!

Mum and June ran to Duke.

“Duke ran off to dig a hole for his bone!” said Mum.

“Duke broke the rules!”

said Mum.

“I cannot be mad at Duke,”

said June.

“He is too **cute**!”

CHECKING FOR MEANING

1. How did Duke get out of the yard? *(Literal)*
2. Where did Mum and June find Duke? *(Literal)*
3. Why did Mum say that Duke broke the rules? *(Inferential)*

EXTENDING VOCABULARY

froze	What happened in the story when Duke froze? *Froze* is the past tense of *freeze*. What else can freeze?
hole	How does Duke make a hole in the story? What word do you make if you replace the letter *l* in the word *hole* with the letter *p*?
cute	Do you think Duke is cute? What are some other words that could be used to describe him?

MOVING BEYOND THE TEXT

1. How can people keep their pets safe?
2. Why is it important to get a tag for pets?
3. What can you train a dog to do?
4. What should you do if you find a lost pet? Why should you tell an adult, rather than approaching a lost pet on your own?

TIME TO WRITE

Imagine you are Duke in the story. Write about his trip to the lake.

PRACTICE WORDS

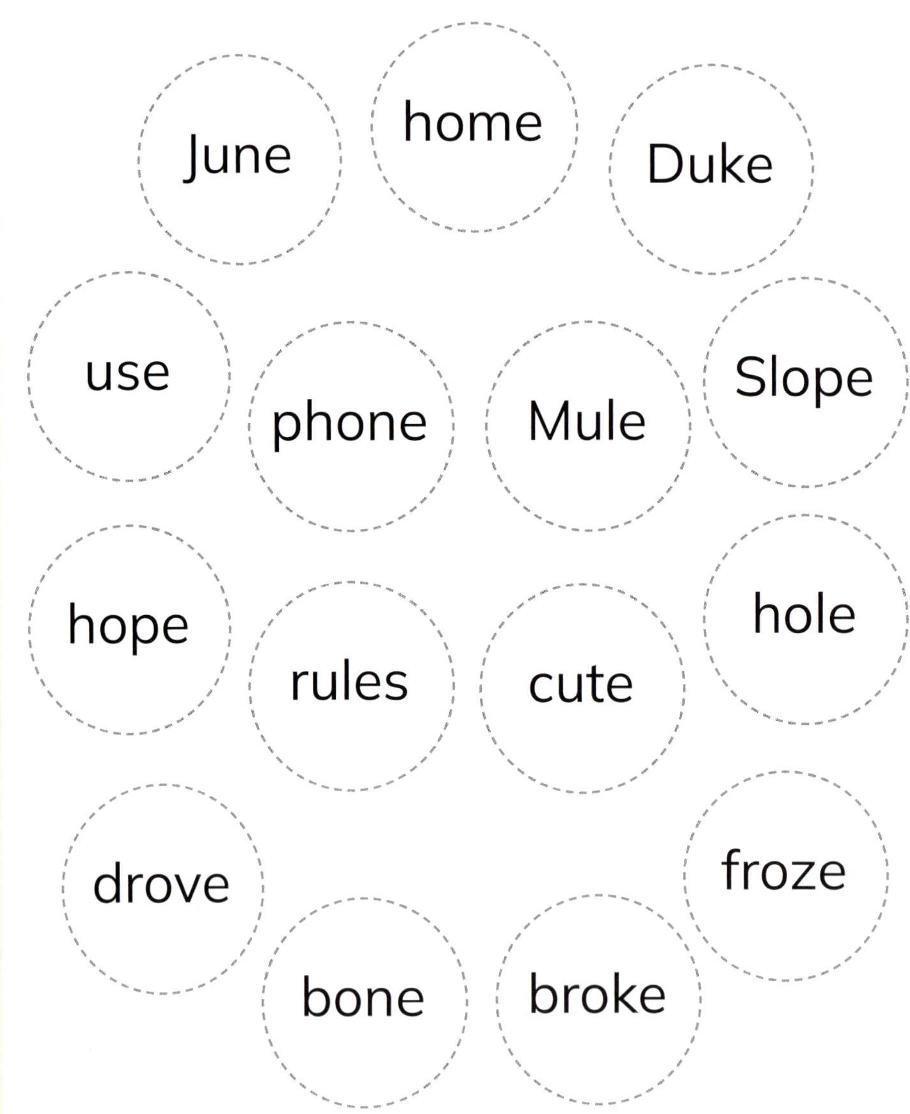